1002
SALT AND PEPPER
Shakers

Sylvia Tompkins

WITH PRICES

- NODDERS
- FITZ AND FLOYD
- PARKCRAFT

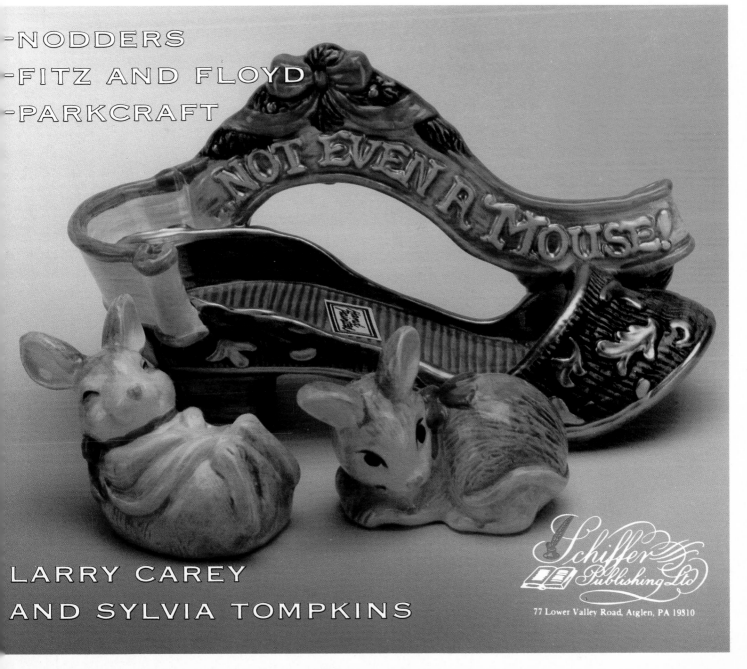

LARRY CAREY
AND SYLVIA TOMPKINS

Schiffer Publishing Ltd

77 Lower Valley Road, Atglen, PA 19310

Dedication

This book is dedicated to Bob and Marianne Ahrold of Burlington, Iowa, Mr. Parkcraft and Mari Jill of Heather House, for their 40 years of contributions to the hobby of novelty salt and pepper collecting.

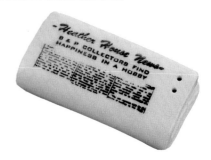

Contents

Copyright © 1995 by
Larry Carey and Sylvia Tompkins

Printed in Hong Kong
ISBN: 0-88740-789-7

We are interested in hearing from authors with book ideas on related topics.

Library of Congress Cataloging-in Publication Data

Carey, Larry
  1002 salt & pepper shakers / Larry Carey & Sylvia Tompkins.
    p.   cm.
  Includes bibliographical references and index.
  ISBN 0-88740-789-7 (soft)
  1. Salt and pepper shakers--Collectors and collecting--United States--Catalogs. I. Tompkins, Sylvia. II. Title.
NK8640.C37   1995
730'.075--dc20   95-6996
                       CIP

Published by Schiffer Publishing Ltd.
77 Lower Valley Road
Atglen, PA 19310
Please write for a free catalog.
This book may be purchased from the publisher.
Please include $2.95 postage.
Try your bookstore first.

Acknowledgments

We greatly appreciate the encouragement and assistance of fellow collectors, and especially the following contributors to this book:

Marianne and Bob Ahrold
Barb Era Beckey
Laura and Richard Bouchard
Cherie Boyer
Frances Clements
Nigel Dalley
Marilyn DiPrima
Joyce & Bill Fisher
Jeanne Fouts
Charlene Green
Marty Grossman
Lorraine Haywood
Joyce Kline
Jean Moon

Hanna O'Clair
Rich O'Donnell
Judy & Jeff Posner
Joanne Rose
Therrie Sherwood
Marcia Smith
Sharon Schwartz
Frances Tawater
Dianne & Tom Thorn
Irene Thornburg
Ruth & Ken Wittlief

We also appreciate the assistance and cooperation of Fitz and Floyd, especially Mr. Kyle Hall of the Public Information Office and Mrs. Kerrie Monti of the Sales Staff, who provided invaluable information included in this book.

Introduction

We appreciate the positive comments we received about our first book. Your favorable responses encouraged us to continue.

Coverage of this second book includes nodders; the evolution of Fitz and Floyd designed S&Ps from early stoneware to today's top of the line sets; and the history and design of Parkcraft shakers. A few sets pictured in our first book have been repeated here, as they fit into more than one category and we are trying to cover each area as completely as possible.

Values are based on our experience and input from contributors. They are intended as a guide only, and will vary depending on condition, geographical area, knowledge of the seller or buyer, and to some extent, on sheer luck.

There are many specialty areas of S&P collecting that can be addressed. Input from collectors on categories to be covered in future books will be greatly appreciated and given serious consideration. We would also welcome additional information on sets in this book.

The 1500 members of the Novelty Salt & Pepper Shakers Club have discovered the enjoyment and benefit to be derived from joining with others who share a love for our hobby. Each year the Club convention is held in a different part of the country to afford the opportunity for attendance to as many members as possible. Our four annual newsletters provide information on shaker identification and history, as well as the chance to buy, sell, and trade. For information about the Club, contact the authors.

Nodders

We have not been able to unearth any information on the origin of nodders, except that most were made in Japan. Despite inquiries to six Japanese patent organizations, no information was obtained. The majority of the nodders are marked Patent TT or Pat TT in raised or incised letters. Any other information or different patent marks are noted.

While the German nodders are pre-WWII, and a few others are comparatively recent, most nodders were produced in the 1950s and 1960s.

Collectors are familiar with the term "common white base" - but did you know there are several variations of this base? Differences exist in the floral design, height, diameter of the holes into which the tubes fit, and the mold of the bottom and sides. See page 33 for a picture showing three of these. Additional base designs are illustrated throughout the book.

Paper decals or stickers shown on some sets do not affect value.

Sitting bears. 3.5". $40-45.

Animals

Running bears. 3.75". Brown, $65-75. Gray, $75-85.

Running bears. 3.75". 1980. Moscow Olympics souvenir base, found in Australia. $250+.

Black cats, same base and Mom shaker. 3.75". Left set, Mom with kitten, $250-275. Right set, Mom with paw, $350+.

"Bobbing Cow Babies." 4". Clay Art, CA. 1994. China. $25.

Cats nod no. 3.5". Left set, $55-60. Right set, $40-45.

Resting camel with monkey shakers. 3.75". $350.+

7

Lying deer. 3.5". $45-50.

Running deer in scenic long base, front and back views. 4".
$90-100.

Running deer. 4". $65-75.

Donkeys. 3.5". $65-75.

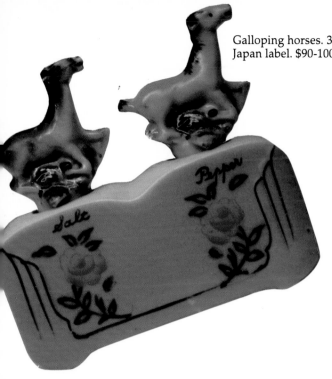

Galloping horses. 3.5". Black and gold Victoria Ceramics, Japan label. $90-100.

Race horse condiment, front and back views. 4". Pat KS. $200-250.

Race horse condiment, front and back views. 4". Pat KS. $200-250.

Walking elephant with clown and dog shakers. 5". $350.+

Small elephants. 2.75". $150-175.

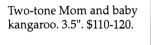

Two-tone Mom and baby kangaroo. 3.5". $110-120.

Two-tone Mom and baby kangaroo. 4.5". Stamped China in red. Apparently distributed primarily in Great Britain. $140-150.

Mom and baby kangaroo. 4". Mom nods yes, baby nods no. Royal Sealy, Japan label. $85-95.

√

Mice outside cheese. Note incised lettering.

"Say Cheese," mouse in cheese base. 3.5". Fitz and Floyd. 1980. Japan. $300-350.

"Hear No Evil, See No Evil, Speak No Evil." 3.25". $300-350.

Monkeys nod yes. 3.5". $90-100.

Monkeys nod no. 3.5". $65-75.

"Hear No Evil, See No Evil, Speak No Evil." 3.5". Composition type pottery. No marks. $300-350.

Mom and baby monkeys, mom nods yes, baby nods no. 3.75".
Shown in three color combinations. All tan, $175-200. All gray,
$200-225. Tan and gray, $250-275.

Single rabbit salt shaker nods on egg cup base. 4". Black and gold label, Sonsco, Japan. $140-150.

Snake. 3.25". Vandor Imports, UT. 1988. Korea. $20-25.

Walking bears, front and back views. 4". Note he is to her left. $400.+

Walking Rabbits. 4". Swing China, Japan label. Right set has green Japan stamp. $350+.

Walking pigs. 3.75"- 4".
$275-300.

"I do, I do." Wedding Pig couple. 3.75". 1980. Fitz and Floyd. Japan. $300-325.

Walking pigs. 3.25". 1980s. Private ceramicist. U.S.A. $125-150.

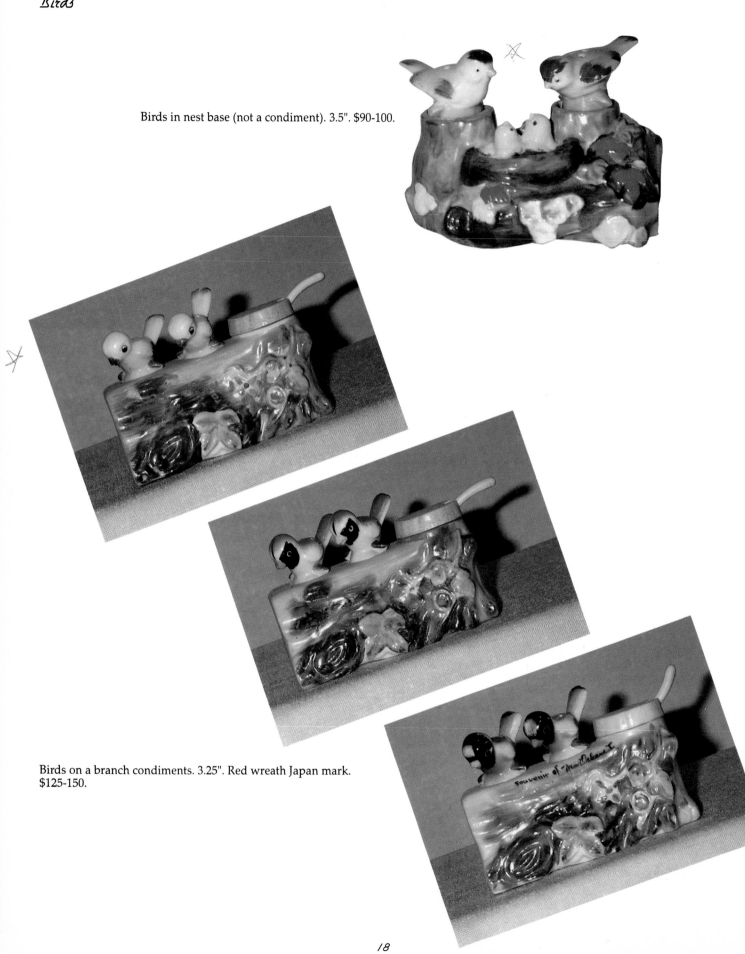

Birds in nest base (not a condiment). 3.5". $90-100.

Birds on a branch condiments. 3.25". Red wreath Japan mark. $125-150.

Canaries. 3.75". Blue and silver label, Enesco Imports. $65-75.

Ceramic version of "Rock a Bye Birdies". 3.5". Red Made in China stamp. Chinese letters. $125-150.

"Rock-a-bye Birdies." 3". Plastic. Chap Stick Co. 1977. Hong Kong. $50-55.

Chickens. 3.5". $35-40.

Blue chickens. 3.5". $75-85.

Three chickens with variations in hole locations: front, top and rear. 3.25". $40-45.

Chickens. 3.25". $35-40.

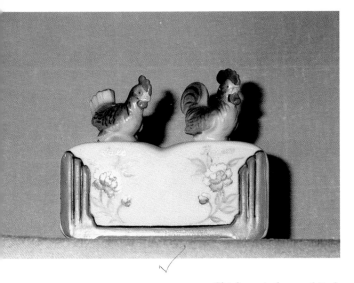 

Chickens in long white base with vertical lines and original
orange/black trim, front and backviews. 3.75". $65-75.

Chickens in Souvenir of Mexico base, front and back views.
3.5". $75-85.

Mark on bottom of base.

Chickens in lustre barrel-like base. 3.25". $75-85.

Chickens in gold and white base. 3.25". $75-85.

Chickens in barrel-like bases with Oriental people design, front and back views. 3.25". $125-150.

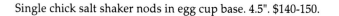

Single chick salt shaker nods in egg cup base. 4.5". $140-150.

Chickens in very unusual base. 4.5". $150-175.

Chicken condiments with floral design bases. 3.5". Some are
Occupied Japan. $75-85.

Front and back views.

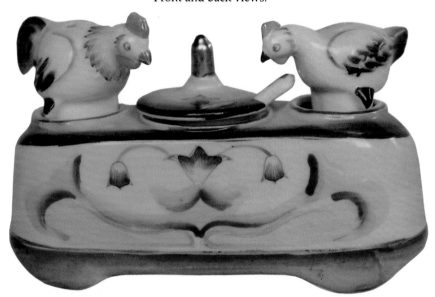

Front and back views.

Chicken condiments, white with gold designs, front and back
views. 3.5". Some are Occupied Japan. $115-125.

Front views only. Same design on back. Right set Pat TK.

Chicken condiment, all gold. 3.5". $250-275.

Chicken condiment with farm scene base. 3.5". Red wreath, Japan. Pat KS. $100-125.

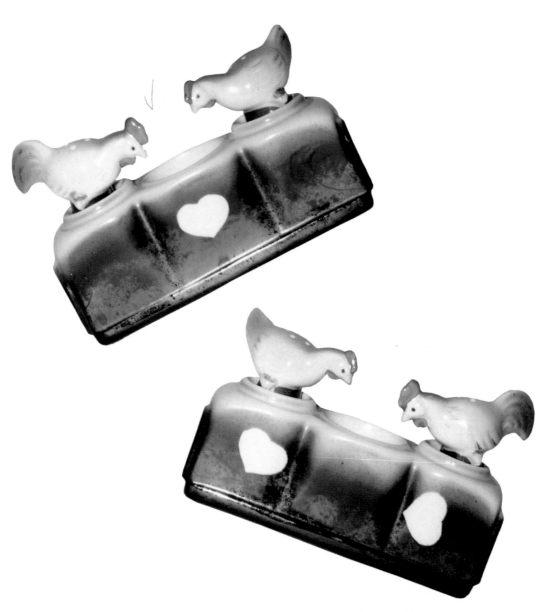

Chicken condiment with heart design base, front and back views. 3.5". If complete, $100-110.

Moriage chicken condiments. 3.5". $115-125.

Chicken condiments in nest base. 4". $90-100.

Satsuma chicken condiments. 3.5". $175-200.

Front and back views.

Ducks. 3 - 3.25". $32-35.

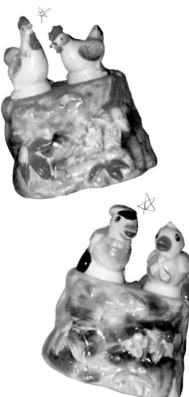

Dressed ducks and chickens in floral nest bases. 4". Left set, green clover leaf Japan; right set red Japan. $75-85.

Flamingos. 3.25". Left set, $45-48. Right set with shell applique, $65-70.

Flamingos in souvenir bases. 3.25". $90-100.

Birds with wires that rest on the base forming the nodder. 4.5"-7". Early 1900s. Germany. Singles, $100-125. Parrots, $175-200. Large birds, $250-300.

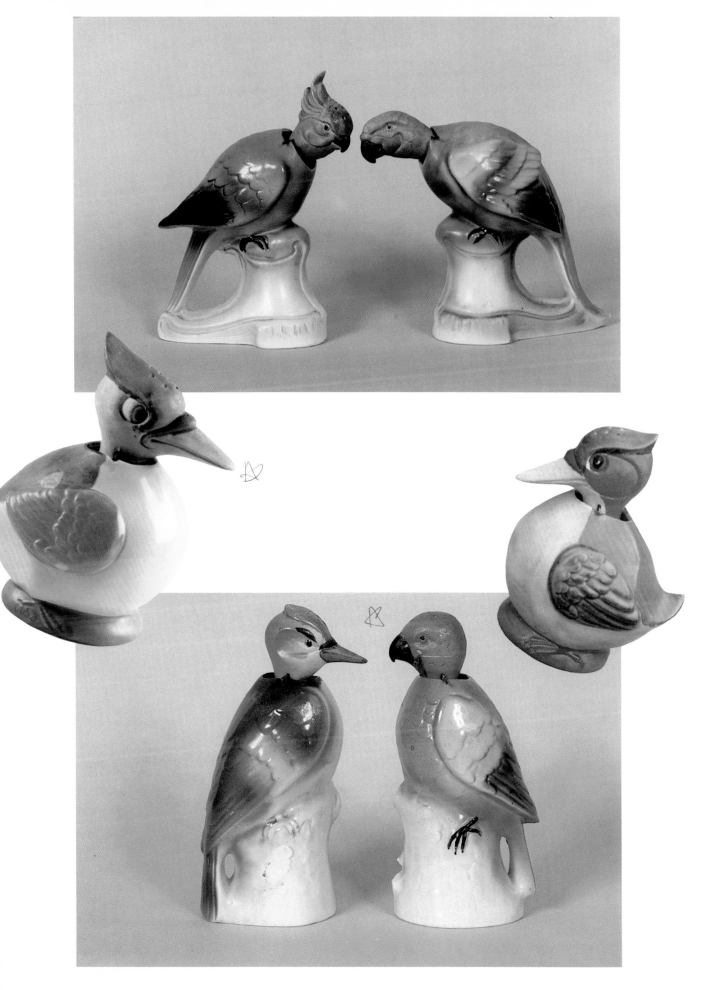

Parakeet condiments. 3". Some are occupied Japan. $90-100.

Satsuma parakeet condiments, front and back views. 3.25".
$150-175.

Pheasants in three types of small, common white base. 3-3.5".
$35-40.

Pheasants. 3.25". $35-40.

Satsuma parakeet condiments, front and back views. 3.25".
$150-175.

Pheasants in raised floral design base. 3.25". Red clover/ wreath mark, Japan. $65-75.

Pheasant condiment. 3.25". $150-175.

Turkey condiment, back and front views. 4". Red wreath mark Japan. $150-175.

Turkeys in raised floral design base. 3". $60-65.

SOUVENIR OF CASA LOMA

Fat Tubes   Nodders with fat tubes in special bases. 3"-3.75". Tubes do not fit in small common white base. Regular nodder tubes are too narrow for these bases. Note variation of flamingo base on right. Some have Kenmar or A Quality Product, Japan label. $70-75.

Most common fish nodders. 3.25". Left set paper label, G Novelty Co., Japan. $32-35.

Fish. 3". $55-60.

Trout. 2.75 - 3.25". $55-60.

Fish. 3.25". Right set has shell applique. $65-75.

Goldfish in barrel shaped base. 2.75". Pat TK. $75-85.

Fish Condiments

Fish Condiments. 3.25". $150-175.

Front and back views.

Occupied Japan.

Occupied Japan.

Occupied Japan.

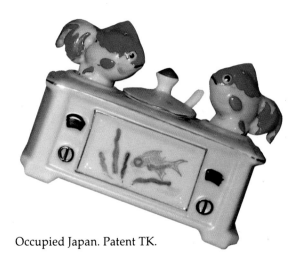

Occupied Japan. Patent TK.

Occupied Japan. Patent TK.

Miniatures

Miniature nodders designed and produced by Laura and Carl Urban of Illinois. 1.5"-2". 1990s. Issue price, $50.

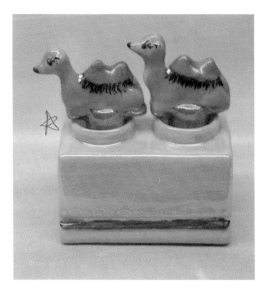

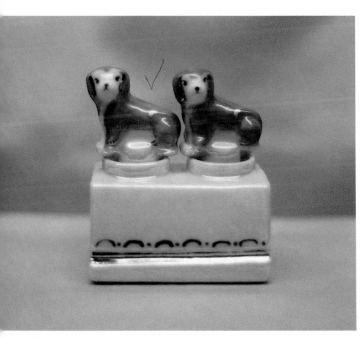

 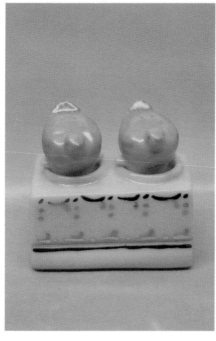 

Black couple, front and back views. Only three sets produced. Sold at 1994 Club Convention Auction for $700.

Series

Shown on the next three pages is a series of eight nodders located to date with special design small white bases. 3.25-3.75". Note that each nodder has a matching figure on the front of the base. Some sides and back are common to more than one set. Front and back views are illustrated. $125-150.

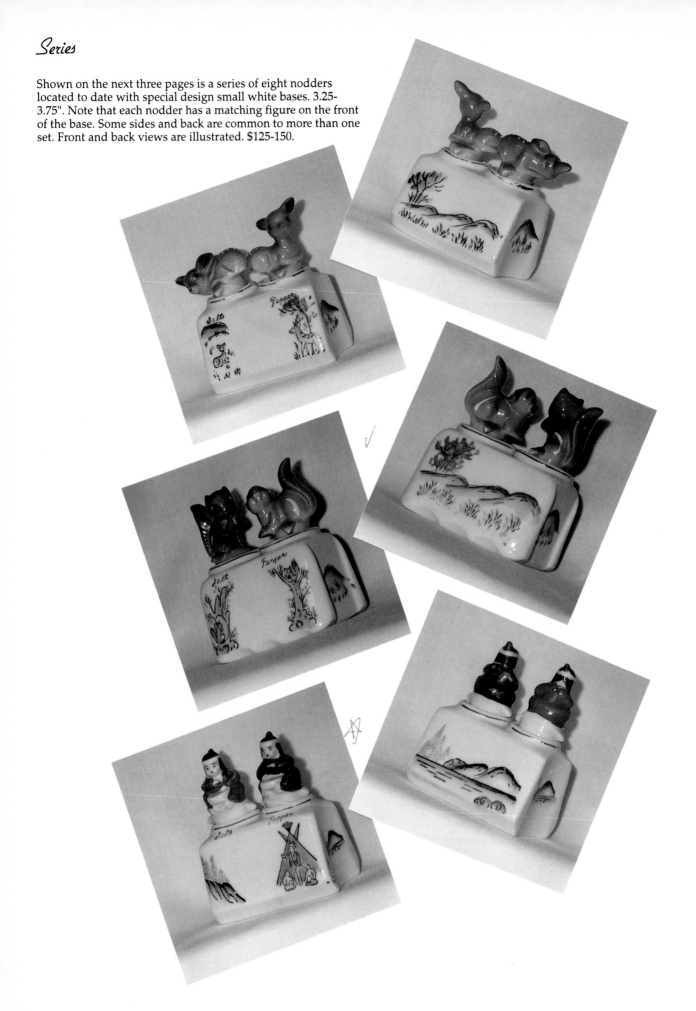

People

"A Nod to Abe". 5.5". The 1991 S&P Club Convention set, designed by Betty Harrington, the primary designer for Ceramic Arts Studio, Madison, WI. Set on left is marked #1 and signed by Betty Harrington. Set on right was available to S&P Club members. 400 sets were produced by Regal China Corp., who ceased business in June 1992. The #1 set sold at the Club Convention Auction for $1100. The set on right originally sold for $35, current value $150-200.

Bottom of #1 set.

Removable hat as a cover

Betty Harrington

45

Black ladies with watermelon. 3.5". Left set, with teeth. Right set, without teeth. $200-250.

Brown lady with watermelon, without teeth. 3.5" $200-250.

Brown lady with watermelon, with teeth, $200-250

Native with white clothing, holding watermelon. 3.5". $200-250.

Black lady with watermelon. 3.5". Brown pottery. No marks. $200-250.

Snake charmer. 3.75". Royal Sealy, Japan label. $350-400.

Snake charmer is darker.

Kissing Dutch couple in long, common white base. 3.25". $75-85.

Kissing Dutch couple in windmill base. 3.25". $125-135.

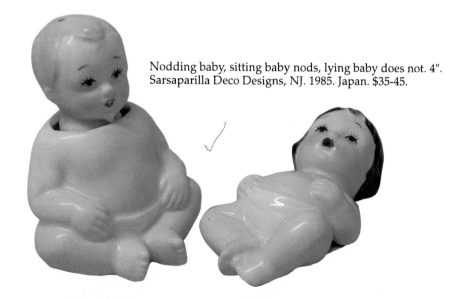

Nodding baby, sitting baby nods, lying baby does not. 4". Sarsaparilla Deco Designs, NJ. 1985. Japan. $35-45.

"Happy and Sad." 3.5". Pat TK, $225-250.

Nude taking bath. 4.75". Legs nod, but are not shakers. $225-250.

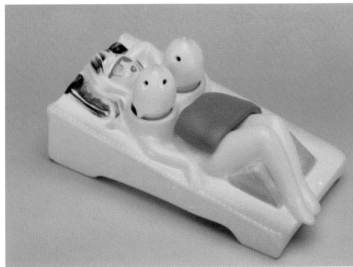

Sunbathing nude condiment. 2.75". Sarsaparilla Deco Designs, NJ. 1980s. Japan. $45-50.

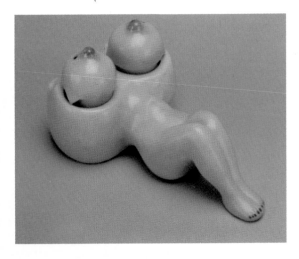

Headless nude. 2.25". $125-150.

Four-eyed couple. 3.25". Couple in barrel nods 'yes'; other couple nods 'no'. Empress, Japan label. 3.25". $100-125.

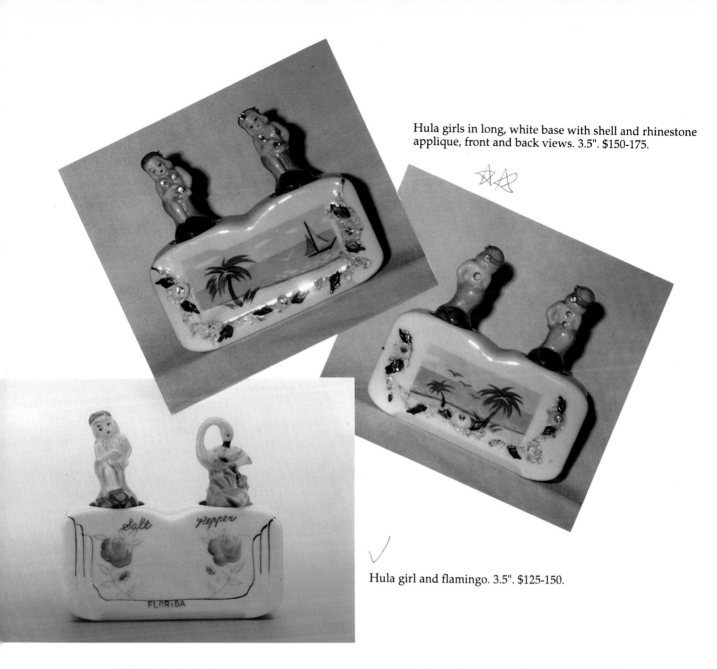

Hula girls in long, white base with shell and rhinestone applique, front and back views. 3.5". $150-175.

Hula girl and flamingo. 3.5". $125-150.

Hula girl with palm tree, and hula girls. Same base, front and back views. 3.5". $125-150.

Indians in drum base with raised Indian designs. 4.25". $100-125.

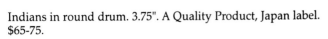

Indians in small white base with special Indian designs, front and back views. 3.75". $90-100.

Indians in round drum. 3.75". A Quality Product, Japan label. $65-75.

Souvenir of Mexico condiments, front and back views. 4".
$150-175.

Oriental nodders. 3.25-3.5". Bottom pictures Moriage, front and back views, black and gold Palmar, Japan label. $225-250.

Red Manna China Kutani stamp. Pat TK.

Irish

Irish couple souvenirs. 3.5"-4". Stamped in red "An tSeapain tir a Dheanta", apparently Gaelic for "Made in Japan for sale in Ireland." $175-200.

Back view.

Irish lady with open salt. 3.25". $150-175.

Full-bodied Irish children. 4.25". Stamped with Gaelic words. $300-350.

Full bodied Irish children in heart-shaped condiment base. 4.25". $400-450.

Rabbits in Irish souvenir base. 3.5". $250-275.

Skulls

Small skulls in variations of small common skull base. 3.5".
$30-35.

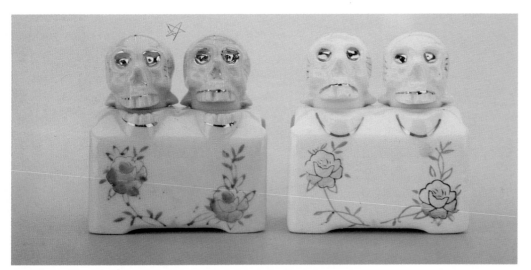

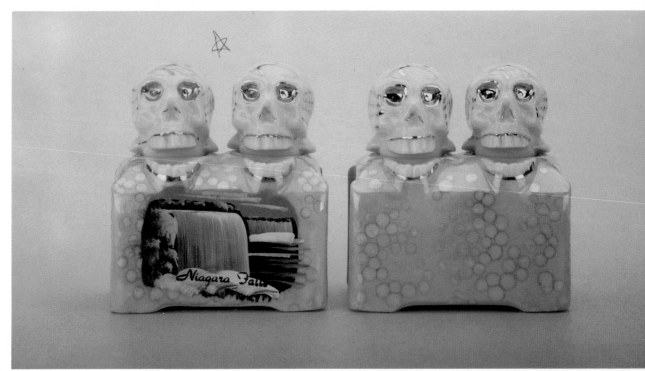

Large skulls in large, heavy bases with lustre, floral or moriage designs. 3.5-3.75". Lustre, $125-150. Floral, $175-200. Moriage, $225-250.

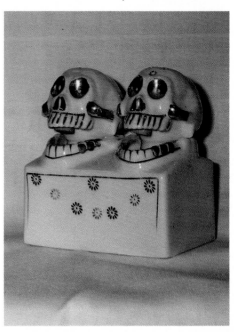

Skulls with raised bones on bisque base, front and back views.
3.25". Rare. $200-225.

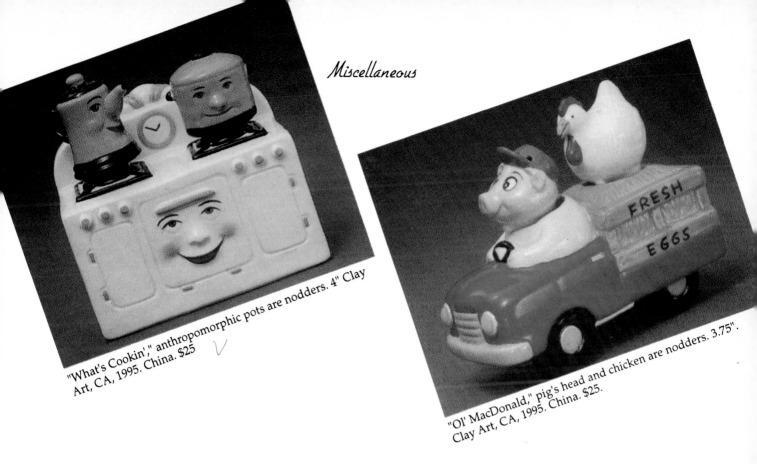

"What's Cookin'," anthropomorphic pots are nodders. 4" Clay Art, CA, 1995. China. $25

"Ol' MacDonald," pig's head and chicken are nodders. 3.75". Clay Art, CA, 1995. China. $25.

Sail boats. 3.75". Left set, $75-85. Right set, $60-65.

Special

SPECIAL NODDERS. This group includes very unusual and rare nodders. A few are one-of-a-kind known to date; some only 2 or 3 have surfaced. Still others were made for markets in other countries and are hard to find in the U.S.

"The Raisin Nodder," No. 1 1988 S&P Club Convention set, front and back views. 5". Sold at Club Convention auction for $450.

"The Raisin Nodder," front and back views. 5". The 1988 Convention set, available to club members. Issue price, $25. Current value, $350+.

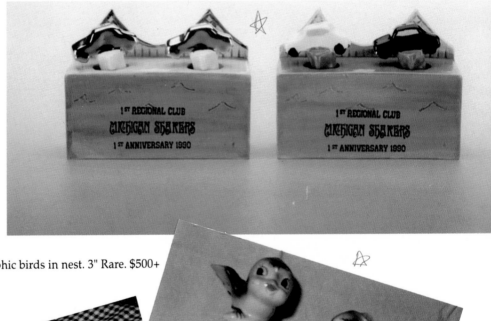

Made for the Michigan Shakers chapter of the S&P Club, 1st anniversary. 3.25". K. Wolfe Studio, MI. 1990. Left set, one of two sets produced with gold and silver cars, $300-350. Right set, available to club members. Issue price, $45. Current value, $175-200.

Anthropomorphic birds in nest. 3" Rare. $500+

Anthropomorphic birds in nest. 3". Found in Australia. Very rare. $600+.

"Huey, Dewey, and Louie." 3.5". Not licensed by Walt Disney. Extremely rare. $800+.

Oriental couple, 3.75" Very rare. $600+.

Rabbits on sofa playing musical instruments. 3.5". Very rare. $600+.

Clowns on circus ball bases. 4". Swing China, Japan. $400-450.

Man feeding squirrel, his head and squirrel nod. 4.75".
Extremely rare. $700+.

Keystone Cop, his head and right hand nod. 5". Very rare.
$600+.

Cowboy. 3.75". $500+.

Boy reading book. 3.75". $350-375.
Book also shown separately.

Butterfly couple, he nods no, she nods yes, front and back views. 4". Stamped Foreign in red. Primarily marketed in Great Britain. $325-350.

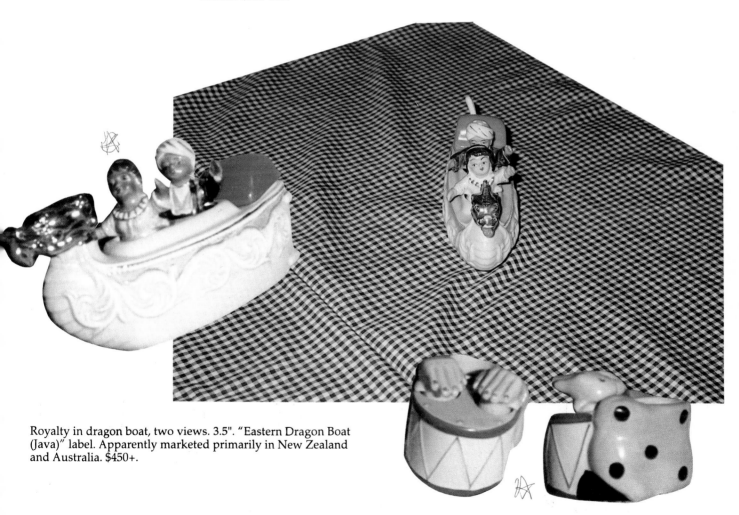

Royalty in dragon boat, two views. 3.5". "Eastern Dragon Boat (Java)" label. Apparently marketed primarily in New Zealand and Australia. $450+.

Bottom only, hands nod, front and side views. Top possibly clown. Does anyone know? Found in England. If complete, $600+.

Minstrels playing musical instruments. 3". Note that each in varying colors is used for two different heads. Both heads with bonnets have 4 holes, one with quite large and one with very small. Rare. Complete set, $500+.

Rockers and Rollers, Bobbers and Weavers

Animal head S&P on 1 piece base with spikes. 4.25". Napco Ceramics. Japan. $100-125.

Nodding donkey carries S&P canisters on removable wire bracket. 5". Ucagco Japan. $75-85.

Nodding dog pulls mustard cart and carries S&P baskets. 3". Pre WWII. Germany. $250+.

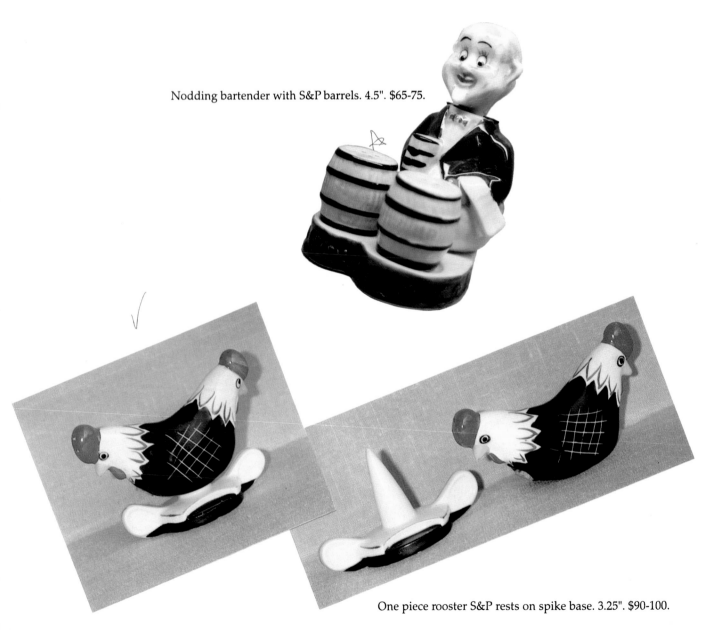

Nodding bartender with S&P barrels. 4.5". $65-75.

One piece rooster S&P rests on spike base. 3.25". $90-100.

Comical dogs with interlocking tails, S&P heads rest on spikes.
4". 1960s. Paper label Japan. Norcrest China, No. H266. $75-85.

Cat head pepper on spike base salt. 3.25"-3.5". $100-125.

Animal cruets (S,P, oil and vinegar). 5-6". Japan. $175-200.

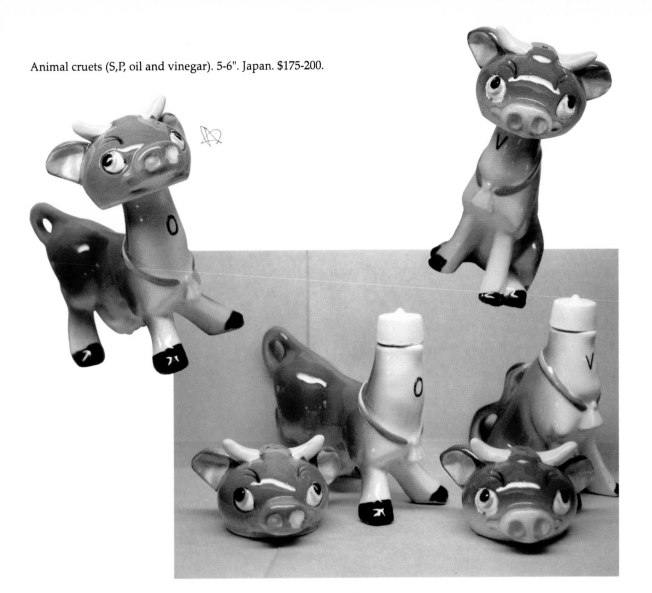

Satsuma Oriental condiment with rounded bottom rocking base. 3". $65-75.

Oriental children with rounded bottom rocking base, two views. 3.5". $50-60.

"Bobbing Siamese Boy 'n Girl," bodies are S&P. 4.25". A Commodore Product, Japan. $35-40.

Fitz and Floyd

Founded in 1960, Fitz and Floyd is widely regarded as the leader in the fashion-forward fine china dinnerware and ceramic giftware segment of the consumer products industry. The company enjoys an outstanding reputation for its exclusive and innovative designs and product quality. Its products are well-established in the marketplace and are retailed through leading specialty and department stores throughout the United States and in international markets.

Dallas, Texas, is home to the acclaimed Fitz and Floyd design staff which creates virtually all of the company's exclusive designs. The relatively new *Fitz and Floyd Heirloom Collectibles* division offers a marvelous variety of limited-edition teapots, figurines, waterballs and annual Christmas ornaments, plates and bells for collectors, many of whom already collected and recognized Fitz and Floyd giftware as "tomorrow's heirlooms today."

In 1993 Silvestri became a division of FFSC, Inc., the parent company of Fitz and Floyd and Omnibus Collection International dinnerware, gourmet accessories and giftware. Silvestri is a leading designer, importer and wholesale distributor of Christmas decorations, seasonal gifts and home decorative accessories.

Fashion quality and innovation have been the key elements that have propelled Fitz and Floyd into a position of leadership in the industry. Fitz and Floyd china and giftware products are visually dramatic and are typically favored by retailers to create high impact attractive displays. The distinctive style of the uniquely designed, detailed and handpainted giftware has earned them a reputation as being virtual "ceramic sculptures."

Many S&P collectors have become interested in Fitz and Floyd shakers due to their originality, quality and "collectability." We therefore decided to feature these S&Ps, showing primarily the older ones and those that are no longer available from the company. We think you will be especially interested in the evolution of F&F salt and peppers from the stoneware sets of the 1960s to the gorgeous Night Before Christmas set shown below.

"Night Before Christmas." 3.5". 1993. Paper label Taiwan. $35-40.

Stoneware cats. 3.25". 1960s. Japan. $35-40.

"Camel." 3 piece. 3.5", 1979. Japan. $55-60.

"Kitten Kaboodle" cats in ceramic basket. 3".
1980. Japan. $55-60.

Cats outside basket.

"Cat's Pajamas." 3.5". Late 1980s. Korea. $32-35.

"Fantasy Fair" cats. 2.5". 1987.
Japan. $35-40.

"Chelsea Cat." 3.5". 1985. Japan. $25-30.

"Courting Kitty Kottage." 4". 1992. Paper label Sri Lanka. $25-30.

"Kittens of Knightsbridge." 4". 1990. Paper label Taiwan. $35-40.

"Steve and Eydie" (dinosaurs). 3.75". 1987. Japan. $35-40.

"Jungle Elephant." 3.5". 1992. Paper label Korea. $30-35.

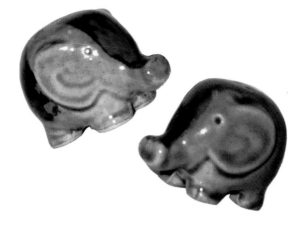

Stoneware elephants. 2.5". 1960s. Japan. $20-25.

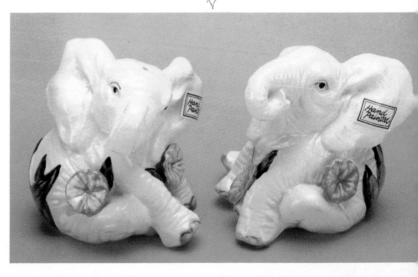

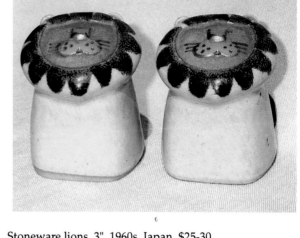

Stoneware lions. 3". 1960s. Japan. $25-30.

"Hippos." 2.75. 1980. Japan. $30-35.

"Lamb." 3". 1983. Japan. $30-35.

"Kangaroo." 4.5". 1978. Japan. $50-55.

"Barnyard Group Lamb." 3.5" 1985. Japan. $30-35.

"Mouse." 2.5". 1979, Japan. $30-35.

"Monkey Love." 3.5". 1978. Japan. $30-35.

"Jungle Monkey." 4". 1991. Paper label Korea. $30-35.

Stoneware pigs. 2". 1960s. Japan. Also produced in black and in dark brown. $20-25.

"Pig." 4.75". 1984. Japan. $35-40.

"Pig Kitchen." 4". 1981. Japan. $35-40.

"Bacon and eggs." 3.75". 1987. Paper label Taiwan. $30-35.

"Kissing Bunny." 4". 1980s. Japan. $35-40. ✓

Bunnies kissing.

Rabbit in hat. 3". Early 1970s. Japan. $45-50.

"Kensington Rabbit." 4.25". 1990. Paper label Taiwan. $30-35.

"Mother Rabbit." 3.5". 1984. Japan. $65-75.

Mother and baby separated.

"Owl and the Pussycat" in a boat. 3.25". 1980. Japan. $65-75.

"Dog/cat," dog with a cat in the tree. 6.25". 1980s. Japan. $45-50.

"Cuddling Pigs." 3". 1976. Japan. $25-30.

"Hampshire Hog." 3.5". 1992. Paper label Taiwan. $35-40.

"Little Mutt." 3". 1981. Japan. $55-60.

"Cat-Nap." 2.25". 1980s. Japan. $25-30.

"Cuddling Ducks". 1.5". 1981. Japan. $20-23.

"Cuddling Owls." 3.5". 1981. Japan. $25-30.

"Cuddling Rabbits." 1.5". 1981. Japan. $20-23.

"Cuddling Lambs." 3". 1981. Japan. $25-30.

"Chicken Coop." 3". 1979. Japan. $45-50.

Chickens outside coop.

"Black and White Lambs" in a wooden trough. 3.25". 1979. Japan. $32-35.

Lambs outside trough.

"Hare and Tortoise" in a wooden trough. 3". 1979. Japan. $32-35.

Hare/tortoise outside trough.

"Pigs in a Poke" (wooden trough). 3.25". 1980s. Japan. $25-28.

Pigs outside poke.

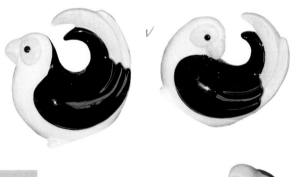

"Bassett Hound." 3". 1982. Japan. $60-65.

"Caribbean Parrot" in different colors. 3". 1979. Japan. $30-35.

"Bird in Hand." 2.5". 1980. Japan. $35-40.

Stoneware birds. 3". 1960s. Japan. $30-35.

"Jungle Cockatiel." 4.75". 1992. Paper label Korea. $30-35.

"Jungle Parrot." 4". 199?
Paper label Korea. $30-

"Poulet" and "Barnyard." 3". 1981. Japan. $30-35.

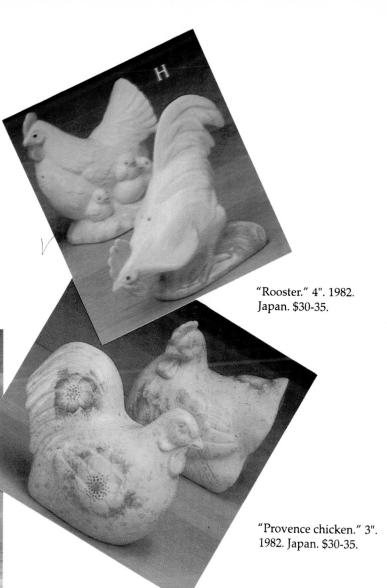

"Rooster." 4". 1982. Japan. $30-35.

"Lecoq." 4.5". 1982. Japan. $30-35.

"Provence chicken." 3". 1982. Japan. $30-35.

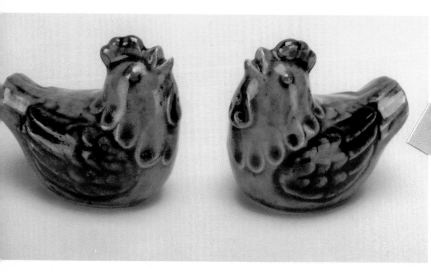

Stoneware chickens. 2.5". 1960s. Paper label Japan. $20-25.

"Country Kitchen Chicken." 3.75". 1985. Japan. $40-45.

Doves. 4". Early 1980s. Japan. $35-40.

"Betty Duck." 4.25". 1985. Japan. $30-35.

"Le Duck." 3.5". 1987. Japan. $30-35.

Quails. 3". 1981. Japan. $20-25.

"Mallard." 2.5". 1987. Japan. $30-35.

"Goony Bird." 2.75". 1980. Japan. $30-35.

Stoneware owls. 2.5". 1960s. Japan. $20-25.

"Owls." 2.5". 1979. Japan. $20-25.

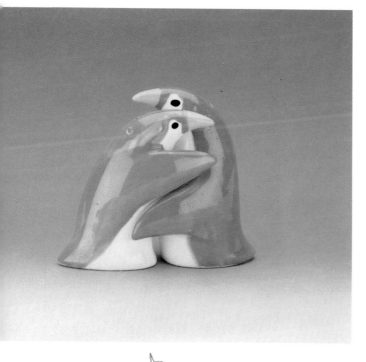

Hugging "Penguins." 2.75". 1981. Japan. $30-35.

"Penguin." 3.75". 1986. Japan. $25-30.

"Swans." 3". 1982. Taiwan. $20-25.

"French Deco Swan." 4.5". 1986. Japan.
Produced in gold, silver, light gray, black and
white. $40-45.

White turkeys. 2.5". 1986. Japan. $30-35.

Deco turkeys. 3.25". 1992. China. Produced as a special order set. $45-50.

"Turkey." 3". 1992. Taiwan. $30-35.

"Canaries in a Cage." 4.5". 1981. Japan. $70-75.

"Jailbirds." 4.5". 1980. Japan. $45-50.

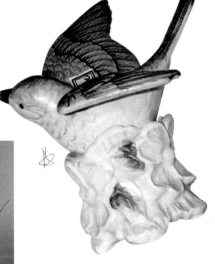

"Nested Love Birds." 3". 1979. Japan. Also produced in pink. $40-45.

"Bluebird." 4.25" 1991. Taiwan. $30-35.

"Rosey Finch." 3.75". 1992. Paper label Taiwan. $30-35.

"Bluebird". 4". 1981. Japan. $40-45.

"Leap Frog." 3.5". 1978. Japan. $30-35.

"Frog." 2.25". 1979. Japan. $20-25.

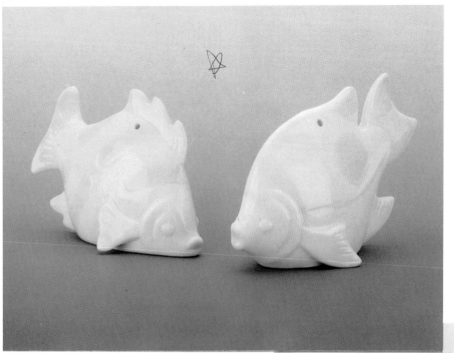

Stoneware snails. 2.5". 1960s. Japan. $20-25.

"Tropical Fish." 2.25". 1981. Japan. $25-30.

"Santa Fe Cactus." 4.5". 1990. Taiwan. $25-30.

"Fish." 2.75". 1978. Japan. $35-40.

"Pansy Parade." 2.25". 1990. Paper label Taiwan. $25-30.

"Sunflower." 2.75". 1988. Japan. $25-30.

"Country Sunflower." 3.75". 1992. Paper label Korea. $25-30.

"Garden Sunflower." 2". 1993. Paper label Taiwan. $25-30.

"April Flowers Pansy." 2.5". 1989. Paper label Japan. $20-25.

"Rose." 3". 1984. Japan. $30-35.

"Fruit Fair" Apple. 2.5". 1991. Paper label Taiwan. $22-25.

"Fruit Fair" Strawberry. 2". 1991. Paper label Taiwan. $22-25.

"Vegetable Harvest" Apple. 3.5". 1990. Taiwan. $22-25.

"Vegetable Garden" Pear. 3.5". 1989. Taiwan. $22-25.

"Fruit Basket Apple." 2.5". 1990. Paper label Taiwan. $22-25.

"Fruit Fair" Lemons. 2.5". 1991. Paper label Taiwan. $70-75

"Fruit Basket Lemons." 2". 1990. Paper label Taiwan. $22-25.

"Vegetable Harvest" Lemon. 2". 1990. Taiwan. $22-25.

"Mediterranean Fruit." 4.5". 1992. Paper label Taiwan. $22-25.

"Fruit Basket Grapes." 3.5". 1990. Paper label Taiwan. $25-30.

"Fruit Basket Oranges." 2.5". 1990. Paper label Taiwan. $22-25.

"Bordeaux grapes." 3". 1990. Paper label Japan. $32-35.

"Artichoke". 3.5". 1991. Paper label Korea. $22-25.

"Asparagus." 3.25". 1988. Paper label Korea. $22-25.

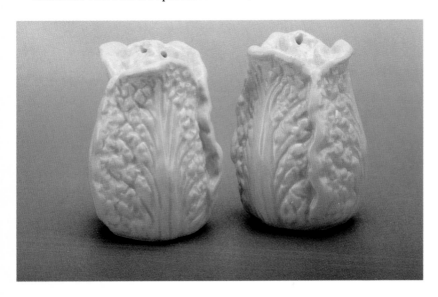

"Cabbage." 3". 1990. Paper label Korea. Probably produced as
a special order set. $18-20.

"Corn." 3". 1982. Japan. $22-25.

"Vegetable Harvest" Cabbage. 3". 1990. Taiwan. $18-20.

"Vegetable Harvest" Cauliflower. 2.75". 1990.
Taiwan. $22-25.

"Eggplant." 3.75". 1991. Paper label Taiwan. $22-25.

"Vegetable Harvest" Eggplant. 3.5". 1990. Taiwan. $18-20.

"Onions." 2.5". 1992. Paper label Philippines. $18-20.

"Onion." 3.5". 1983. Japan. $22-25.

"Vegetable." 3.5". 1982. Paper label Taiwan. $22-25.

"Vegetable Harvest" Garlic. 2.5" 1990. Taiwan. $18-20.

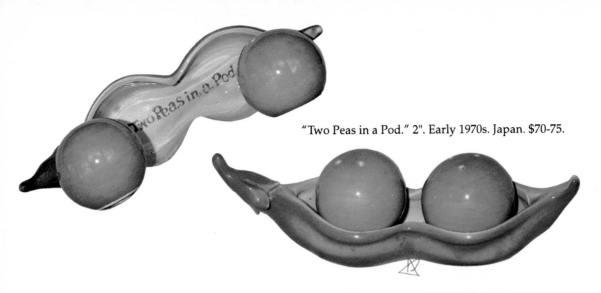

"Two Peas in a Pod." 2". Early 1970s. Japan. $70-75.

"Chili pepper." 2". 1991. Paper label Philippines. $22-25.

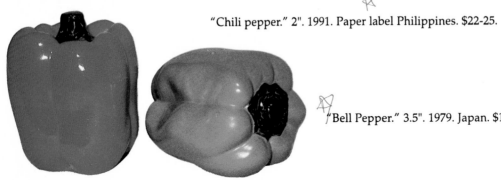

"Bell Pepper." 3.5". 1979. Japan. $18-20.

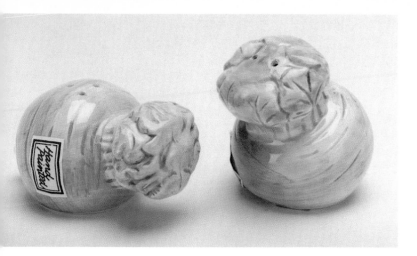

"Radish." 2.5". 1984. Paper label Taiwan. $18-20.

"Kitchen Harvest." 4.5". 1985. Paper label Korea. $18-20.

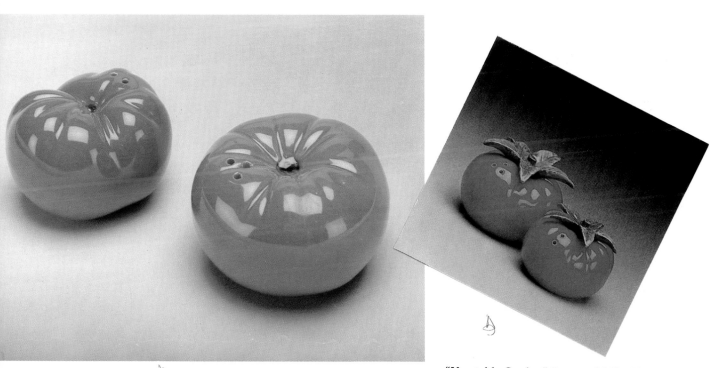

"Tomato." 2". 1992. Paper label Philippines. $18-20.

"Vegetable Garden" Tomato. 2.25". 1989. Taiwan. $22-25.

Stoneware children with balloons. 7". 1960s. Japan. $50-60.

Stoneware children. 4". 1960s. Japan. $40-45.

Indians in a canoe. 3.25". 1981. Japan. $60-65.

"French Chef." 4". 1982. Japan. $40-45.

"Lucky Pierre." Stoneware. 2.5". 1984. Japan. $30-35.

Stoneware bride and groom. 3.5". 1960s. Japan. $40-45.

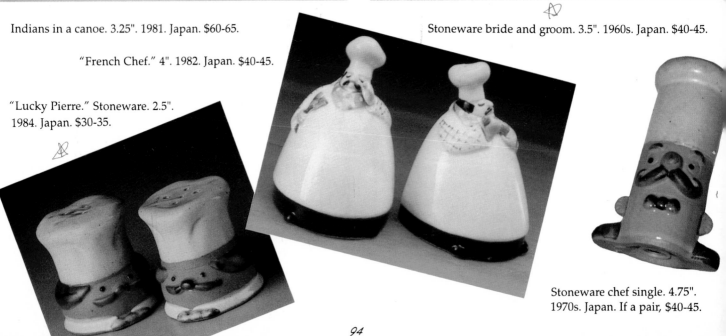

Stoneware chef single. 4.75". 1970s. Japan. If a pair, $40-45.

Topper and hat separated.

"Topper." 4". 1980. Japan. $65-75.

"Seasoned Kissers." 3". 1979. Japan. $50-60.

Cowboy and hat separated.

Mermaids. 2.5". 1981. Japan. $65-75.

"Cowboy." 4". 1980. Japan. $65-75.

"Chip and Cookie." 3.5". 1992. Indonesia. Licensed by Famous Amos Cookies. $35-40.

"Rio Rita." 4". 1989. Paper label Taiwan. $90-100.

Mushrooms, wood. 2". 1960s. Japan. $8-10.

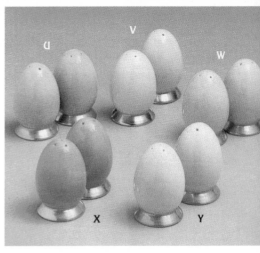

"Pedestal Egg." 2.75". 1983. Japan. $12-15.

Eggs. 1.5". 1970s. Japan. $8.

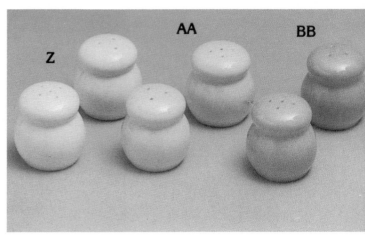

"Total Color Mushroom." 2". 1983. Japan. Variety of colors. $12-15.

"Temple Shaped." 2.75". 1983. Japan. Variety of colors. $12-15.

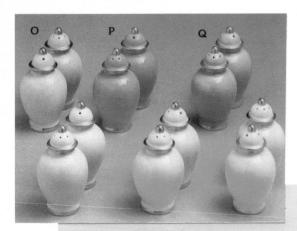

"Total Color Shell." 1". 1986. Japan. Issued in fifteen different colors. $12-15.

Stacking "Pagoda." 4.25". 1980. Japan. Also produced in white. $40-45.

"Coral Shells." 3.5". 1989. Japan. $25-30.

"Oceana" sea shells. 3.25". 1980s. Japan. $22-25.

"Woodland Partridge." 3". 1991. Paper label Taiwan. $30-35.

"Shaughnessy's Little People." 4.25". 1989. Taiwan. $55-60.

"Jack-o-Lantern and Cat." 2.25". 1988. Paper label Japan. $25-30.

"Winter Fruit." 4". 1993. Paper label Taiwan. $30-35

"Kitchen Witch" and caldron. 3.5". 1981. Japan. $40-45.

"Staffordshire Christmas" dogs. 4". 1992. Paper label Japan. $25-30.

"Old World Christmas Bunny." 3.5" 1990. Taiwan. $25-30.

"Holiday Cat." 4.25". 1992. Paper label Taiwan. $25-30.

"Plaid Teddy." 3.5". 1991. Paper label Korea. $25-30.

"Santa Bearhugs." 3". 1984. Japan. $30-35. ✓

Christmas mice. 3". 1992. Taiwan. Probably produced as a special order set. $35-40. ✓

"Christmas Elephant." 3". 1983. Japan. $35-40. ✓

"Snowman." 4.25". 1991. Paper label Korea. $25-30.

"Old World Santa" and bag. 4.25".
1989. Paper label Korea. $30-35.

"Santa's Helpers." 3.5". 1992. Paper
label Taiwan. $25-30.

"Hugging Santa/Rudolph." 3". 1978.
Japan. $35-40.

"Old World Christmas Elves." 3.75". 1990. Paper label Taiwan.
$25-30.

Parkcraft

The company was founded in the late 1940s by Bob and Marianne Ahrold of Burlington, Iowa. Named for a famous park in Burlington, Parkcraft served as design and management head of a multi-faceted business which also included Heather House as a retail mail order operation, Flint Hills Specialty Co. as wholesale, and Riverside Sales for state fairs. Two ladies from Quincy, Illinois, carved models based on Bob's designs. Molds from these models were prepared by the Taneycomo Ceramic Company, Hollister, Missouri (across the river from Branson which then had *one* hotel!) Salt and pepper sets were produced by Taneycomo for Parkcraft, the first one being the ghost and the tombstone "I wuz Pepper".

In about 1950, Bob designed the first three states: Illinois, Iowa, and Missouri, as these were the primary markets. Nine contiguous states followed. Ultimately, all 48 and then 50 states were produced. Initially, several states were made with the same matching object for cost containment reasons. Bob subsequently sent inquiries to each State House as to what object best symbolized that state. These suggestions were incorporated into the 50 state series which had a different object for each state. States originally sold for $1.25, including postage; as late as 1981 they were only $1.50.

As salt and peppers gained in popularity resulting in increased sales, new designs were added. These included the 12 Months of the Year, 18 Famous Cities and 7 Famous People. According to Bob, the 12 months were originally designed and produced with an open book accompanying the matching object. (See page 112). As not many of these sets have surfaced, we believe that production with the books was limited because the design was changed to a column with the matching object. The book design was then used for the 18 Famous Cities series.

As the states and objects have been pictured in previous books, we are not repeating these, but are focusing on other series and lesser known Parkcraft sets. However, discussion on the "three generations" of states is appropriate. (Shown below). The left state is from an original Taneycomo mold. While Taneycomo was owned by Sam Weaver, new molds were prepared as needed to maintain a high quality.

When Taneycomo was acquired by Mrs. Pryor, replacement molds were not produced to sustain the original standards. This deterioration is illustrated by the center state. A third owner continued to use worn molds, thereby further contributing to the deterioration shown by the state on the right. The first generation has an unglazed bottom and is usually stamped Parkcraft. Scotch tape was often placed over the hole, leaving a distinctive residue. Second and third generation states have a slight glaze or sheen on the bottom, may or may not be stamped, and do not show tape residue.

Several S&P series and/or sets have been attributed to Parkcraft that were designed by Bob but not produced by Taneycomo. These include the 7 Days of the Week, Miniature Bone China Nursery Rhymes, Miniature Bone China Animals and President S&Ps. These and many other sets, such as the Surprise of the Month, were offered for sale by Heather House.

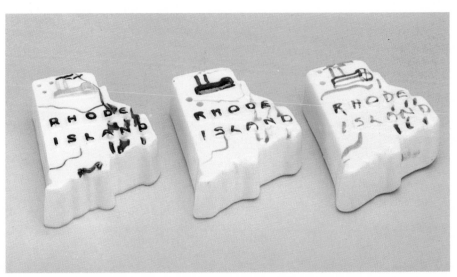

Three generations of Parkcraft States. 3.25".

American and Confederate flags. 2.25". $65-75.

Republican elephant and Democratic mule. 3.25". Mule also matched with the state of Missouri. Elephant matched with another elephant as a separate set. $25-30.

Pair of Republican elephants. 3.25". $25-30.

Bean pots. 2". Note: this is the same pot used with the state of Massachusetts. This set has two and three holes. $15-20.

Pair of oil wells as souvenirs of Hot Springs, AR. 3.5". Oil well also matched with state of North Dakota. $20-25.

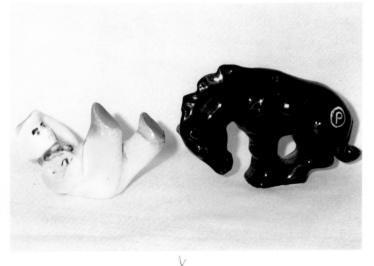

Cowboy and bucking bronco. 3". Bronco also matched with state of Wyoming. $30-35.

Pair of fish, also matched with state of Florida. 2.25". $30-35.

Pheasants. 2.75". Note: large pheasant is also used with the state of South Dakota. Indian and canoe. 3.5". Note: canoe also used with the state of Minnesota. $25-30.

Snowman and sled. 2.25". Snowman also matched with month of February. $35-40.

Squirrel and acorn. 2.25". $12-15.

Skunks. 2". $6-8.

Rabbit and cabbage. 3.75". Cat and ball of yarn. 2.25". $22-25.

Black and white sheep. 2.5". $18-20.

Tom Sawyer and fence. 2.5". Huck Finn on raft. 2.75". $45-

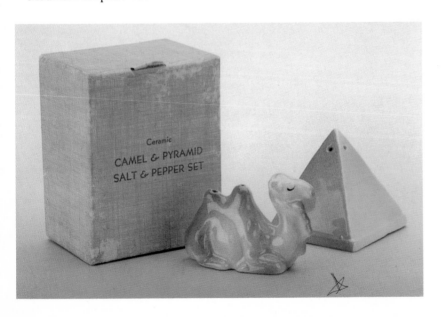

Mountain couple. 3". $25-30.

Porter and suitcase. 2.75" 1950s. $90-100.

Camel and pyramid with original box. 2". $35-40.

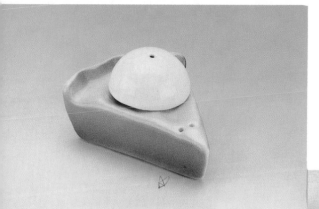

Pie ala mode. 1.5". $12-15.

Tractor and barn, 2". Sock in shoe, 2.5". $35-40.

"Heather House News" and milk bottle. 3". More common paper titled "Morning News." $35-40.

Ghost and tombstone. 2". Shaving brush and mug. 2.5". $15-20.

"Ma" and "Pa" jugs. 2". $12-15.

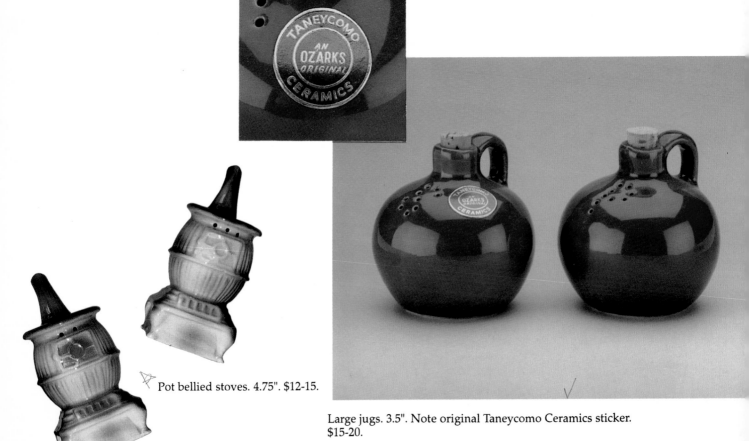

Pot bellied stoves. 4.75". $12-15.

Large jugs. 3.5". Note original Taneycomo Ceramics sticker. $15-20.

Seven Famous People. 2.75"-3.25". $35-40.

George Washington and Will Rogers.

Christopher Columbus and Buffalo Bill.

Charles Lindbergh and Betsy Ross.

Benjamin Franklin.

Twelve Months of the Year. 3.25". $30-35.

January/February.

 March/April.

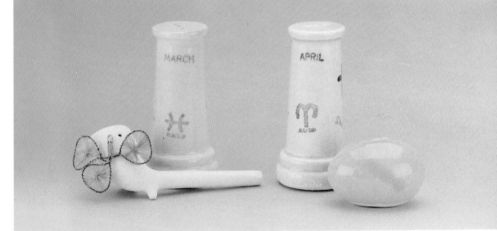

May/June.

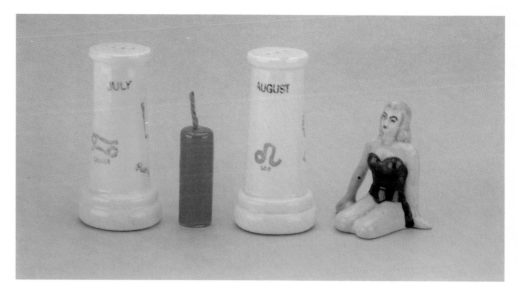

July / August.

September / October.

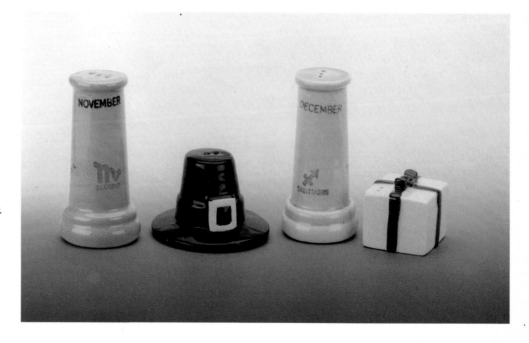

November / December.

Twelve months as originally produced. Each set, $55-60.

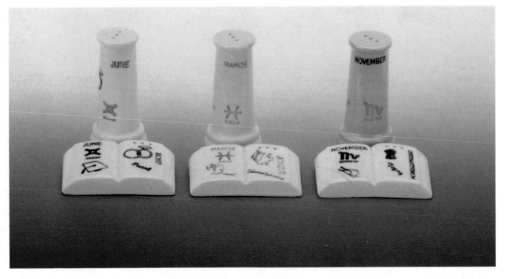

A comparison of the books with symbols as originally produced with the more common columns.